Printed in Great Britain
by Amazon

77799541R00071